The best wo in the world

Bess was a black and white dog who never stopped barking.
She barked at the postman and the milkman.
She even barked at the window cleaner.

"Bess barks at everybody," said Clive.
"She's the best watchdog in the world."

Then one day Bess barked at Miss Brown.

Miss Brown was very cross.
She got a stick and she waved it at Bess.
"Be quiet, you bad dog!" she shouted.

Bess looked at the stick.
She stopped barking and she crept under the table.
She didn't come out all day,
and she didn't bark at all.

At teatime Bess wouldn't eat.
"What's up with Bess?" said Mum.
"She's upset because Miss Brown shouted at her," said Clive.

Clive went out into the street.
"Please come to the door," he said to the postman and the milkman.
"Bess has lost her bark."

The postman and the milkman went
Bang! Bang! Bang! at the door.
"Bark at them, Bess," said Dad.
But still Bess didn't bark.

"Please come to the window," said Clive to the window cleaner.
"Bess has lost her bark."

The window cleaner went to the window but Bess didn't bark at him.
Mum was very upset.
"I'm going to call the vet," she said.

Bess didn't even bark at the vet.
"What shall we do?" said Clive.
"She isn't a good watchdog now."
"She will find her bark again," said the vet.

At bedtime, everybody went to bed.
Nobody saw who was in Miss Brown's garden.

Later, Miss Brown sat up.
A burglar was at the window.
He was trying to get in.
"Help! A burglar!" she shouted.

Bess jumped up and ran.

She ran out of the kitchen and into
Miss Brown's garden

Bess pulled the burglar down.
Miss Brown called the police.

A policeman came and Bess barked at him.
"Don't bark at me, I'm a policeman," said the policeman.
"Bess barks at everybody," said Miss Brown.
"She's the best watchdog in the world."